Researching Online

Ann Truesdell and
John Willis

DIGITAL CITIZENSHIP

LIGHTBOX
openlightbox.com

Go to
www.openlightbox.com
and enter this book's
unique code.

ACCESS CODE
LBXZ9869

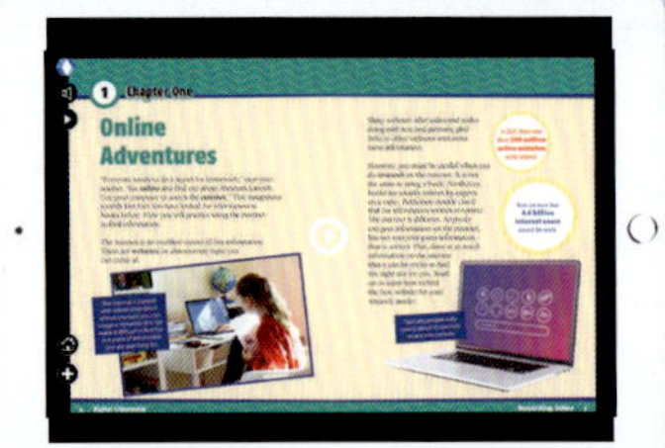

Lightbox is an all-inclusive digital solution for the teaching and learning of curriculum topics in an original, groundbreaking way. Lightbox is based on National Curriculum Standards.

LIGHTBOX SUPPLEMENTARY RESOURCES

SHARE Share titles within your Learning Management System (LMS) or Library Circulation System

CURRICULUM Find national and state curriculum correlations

CITATION Create bibliographical references following the Chicago Manual of Style

STANDARD FEATURES OF LIGHTBOX

AUDIO High-quality narration using text-to-speech system

ACTIVITIES Printable PDFs that can be emailed and graded

SLIDESHOWS Pictorial overviews of key concepts

VIDEOS Embedded high-definition video clips

WEBLINKS Curated links to external, child-safe resources

TRANSPARENCIES Step-by-step layering of maps, diagrams, charts, and timelines

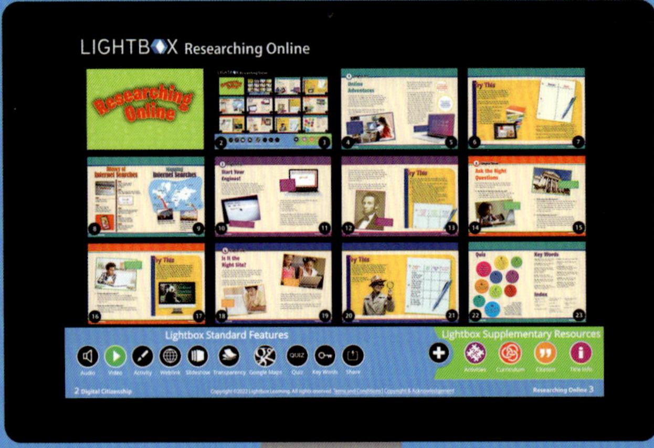

INTERACTIVE MAPS Interactive maps and aerial satellite imagery

QUIZZES Ten multiple-choice questions that are automatically graded and emailed for teacher assessment

KEY WORDS Matching key concepts to their definitions

Researching Online

Contents

1 Chapter One

Online Adventures

"Everyone needs to do a report for homework," says your teacher. "Go **online** and find out about Abraham Lincoln. Use your computer to search the **internet**." This assignment sounds like fun! You have looked for information in books before. Now you will practice using the internet to find information.

The internet is an excellent source of free information. There are **websites** on almost every topic you can think of.

The internet is packed with information about almost any topic you can imagine. However, this can make it difficult to find the one piece of information you are searching for.

Many websites offer video and audio along with text and pictures, plus links to other websites with even more information.

In 2020, there were about **200 million active websites** on the internet.

However, you must be careful when you do **research** on the internet. It is not the same as using a book. Nonfiction books are usually written by experts on a topic. Publishers double check that the information written is correct. The internet is different. Anybody can post information on the internet, but not everyone posts information that is correct. Plus, there is so much information on the internet that it can be tricky to find the right site for you. Read on to learn how to find the best website for your research needs!

There are more than **4.6 billion internet users** around the world.

Typically, people only spend about 45 seconds on any one website.

Try This

Books and the internet are two very different resources, but one is not better than the other. You will choose when to use the internet versus a book depending on what you are looking for and what options you have.

See if you can figure out which resource would be better for you to use in the situations below.

1. Your teacher says to find an article on a current event.
2. You want to find out more about your favorite TV show.
3. You need information about an animal for a research report and you want to make sure that the information is true.
4. You would like to watch a video to learn more about a topic.

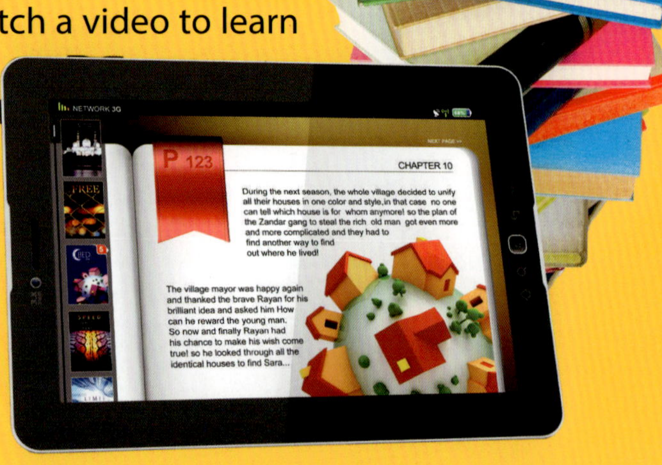

Internet

Book

ANSWERS:

1. The internet changes every second. New articles and websites are always being posted. This makes the internet a great resource for current events.
2. The internet is a great resource for topics that might not have a book written about them, such as TV shows.
3. Books are more likely to be written by an expert than websites. The facts in books are also double-checked by the publisher. You have to be careful when you use a website for information. You have to decide if the site looks trustworthy on your own.
4. The internet has many websites that feature videos to help you learn about a topic, but not all of them are trustworthy.

History of Internet Searches

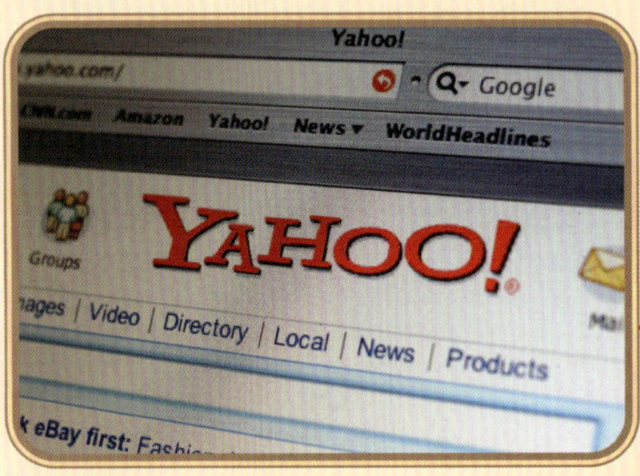

1990
The first simple **search engine**, called Archie, is created.

1994
The Yahoo! search engine includes written **descriptions** of each website.

1998
The search engine Google is launched.

2005
Major search engines begin to take steps to stop low-quality sites from showing up in searches.

2013
Google becomes the first search engine to try to understand the intent behind a search.

2015
Major search engines update to prioritize more mobile-friendly websites

2020
More than half of all web searches are done on mobile devices.

Mapping Internet Searches

Mountain View, California, 2004
Google opens its new headquarters.

Canberra, Australia, 2020
The Australian government begins working on laws requiring search engines to pay for showing news articles.

2 Chapter Two

Start Your Engines!

It is time to do your online research about Abraham Lincoln. Start by using a search engine. A search engine is a computer program that helps you find words or information. You type in words you are searching for. A search engine looks on the internet. It works to find matches for those words. The matches, or results, are called websites.

If you know the address of a website, you can access it directly through your internet browser rather than searching for it.

There are search engines for doing all kinds of research. Some good search engines for kids are:

- www.kidrex.org
- www.kiddle.co
- http://kidsclick.org
- https://wackysafe.com

Suppose you begin your search by carefully typing in "Lincoln." (It is important to spell your search words correctly.) Your search will probably turn up millions of results! The sites will not only be about Abraham Lincoln. Cities that are named Lincoln will show up, too. You will even get sites about cars!

You will have to narrow your search. You only want information about the U.S. president Abraham Lincoln. This time, type in "Abraham Lincoln." A list of thousands of new sites will pop up. But now they are only about Lincoln himself. Each site listed will have a brief description of itself.

Now it is time to do some clever detective work. You can do different searches to find different information about Lincoln. Let us find the right sites for your report!

Well-known topics, such as "Abraham Lincoln," will have far more results than topics that are not as famous.

Try This

What if you change your search words a little? You will get different search results. Let us search for three slightly different subjects.

1. Take out your pencil and notebook. Use a ruler to draw three long lines down one page.
2. Write "Abraham Lincoln speech" at the top of the first column. Write "Abraham Lincoln president" at the top of the second column. Write "Abraham Lincoln politician" at the top of the third column.
3. Do an internet search for each of those three subjects. Look at the results of each search. Write down the first three sites that come up in each search.
4. Do you notice any differences in each search? What other search words could you have used?

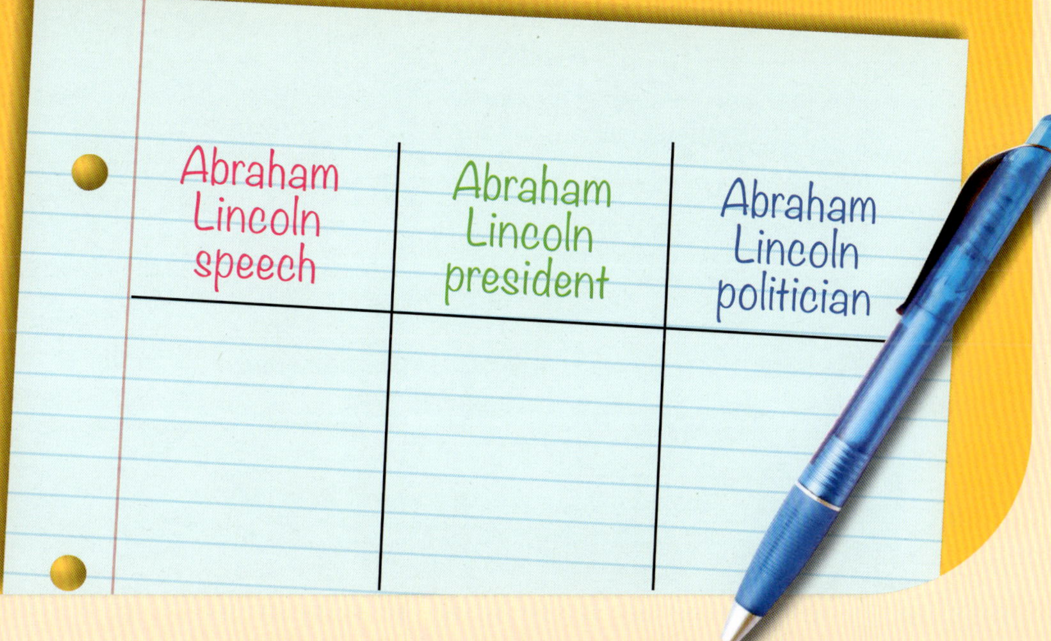

3 Chapter Three

Ask the Right Questions

Look at the different sites on your list. Read the brief descriptions. You want to find the most helpful sites. Ask yourself these questions:

- **"Is the site written for someone my age?"**
  You want to understand what is written. Then the site will be **valuable** to you. Cannot understand it? Then the site is probably meant for older students.

Some encyclopedias also have "kid" versions that are easier for younger readers to understand.

Official websites from trustworthy organizations, such as museums and governments, are typically reliable.

- **"Who wrote the information?"**
  Most **reliable** websites tell you who wrote the information. Is the author an **authority** on the subject? Search the author's name on the internet. You can learn more about his or her **qualifications**. Sometimes organizations are related to the subject. Their websites will often have the best information.

- **"Is the information correct?"**
  Say one site says that Lincoln was from Russia. Stop right there! Visit a few other sites. Learn where they say Lincoln was born. Look at an encyclopedia or a book. The information should all be the same. That first site was the only one to mention Russia. So you know you cannot trust that site.

Visiting a site's references is often a good way to find more books or websites relating to a topic.

- **"Is the information current?"**
  A website often tells you when it was last **updated**. Information changes over time. Facts about Lincoln are found on history sites. History sites should be updated every 5 years.

- **"Does the site list other references?"**
  The author got information from **references**. References are books, articles, or other websites. Most good websites will list those references.

Try This

Test your skills as a website detective. Find a site about your favorite animal. Read an article on that site. What is the name of the author? Is that person an authority on the animal? How would you find out? Does the site say when it was last updated? Does the site list other references? Say you have to write a report on this animal. Would you use this site to do your research? Why or why not?

4 Chapter Four

Is It the Right Site?

You are ready to decide which sites to use for your research. Sometimes a site looks great. However, maybe not all your questions were answered. That site might not be complete. It might be a poor choice for your research.

Sometimes, a website can be misleading. It might have been updated this year. But it still contains information that is wrong. You should find better choices.

Finding a piece of information on just one site may mean that it is incorrect.

You can bookmark particularly useful sites to easily return to them later.

Think about all the questions you asked. Make sure the site meets your needs. One site may not answer all your research questions. Then you will need more than one site. That will give you the best information for your report.

You will have to do online research more and more. Use the tools you learned here every time. You will soon become an authority at finding the best sites.

Try This

Smart detectives take notes. So do smart researchers! Take notes about the websites you visit. Get out a sheet of paper. Make a checklist like the one on the opposite page. Think about each site. Answer each question. Does this information make you want to use the website?

Now put it all together. Will you use any of the sites? Why or why not?

Questions to Ask	Yes? No?	Use the Site	Do not Use the Site
Is the website about your topic?			
Is the website easy for you to read and understand?			
Do the facts seem to be correct?			
Is the writer an authority on the topic?			

Quiz

1
What kinds of topics will often lead to many search results?

2
How many active websites were on the internet in 2020?

3
What is a search engine?

4
Who can post information on the internet?

5
How often should history websites be updated?

6
In what year was Google launched?

7
How many internet users are there?

8
Which websites are typically reliable?

9
What was the first search engine called?

10
How much time do people usually spend on a website?

Answers: 1. Popular ones **2.** About 200 million **3.** A computer program that helps you find words or information **4.** Anyone **5.** Every 5 years **6.** 1998 **7.** More than 4.6 billion **8.** Official websites from trustworthy organizations such as museums and governments **9.** Archie **10.** About 45 seconds

Key Words

authority: someone who is skilled or knows a lot about a subject

descriptions: words or sentences that tell about something

internet: the electronic network that allows millions of computers around the world to connect together

online: connected to other computers through the internet

qualifications: skills or abilities that make someone able to do a job or task

references: books, websites, magazines, or other types of works used to find information

reliable: trustworthy or dependable

research: to look for information on a topic

search engine: a computer program that helps you find words or information you request

updated: changed something, such as a website, in order to include the latest information

valuable: important in some way, such as important information

websites: connected groups of pages on the internet, usually about a single topic or several closely related topics

Index

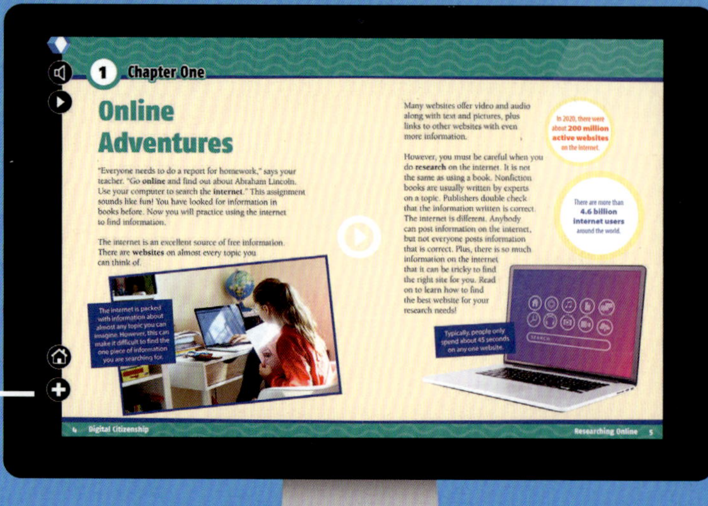

SUPPLEMENTARY RESOURCES

Click on the plus icon found in the bottom left corner of each spread to open additional teacher resources.

- Download and print the book's quizzes and activities
- Access curriculum correlations
- Explore additional web applications that enhance the Lightbox experience

LIGHTBOX DIGITAL TITLES
Packed full of integrated media

VIDEOS

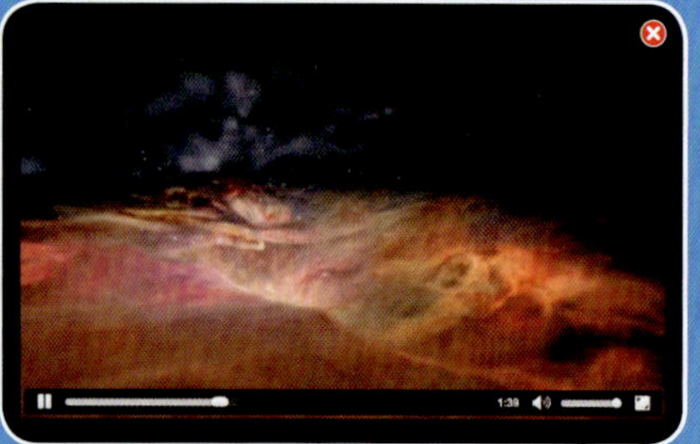

INTERACTIVE MAPS

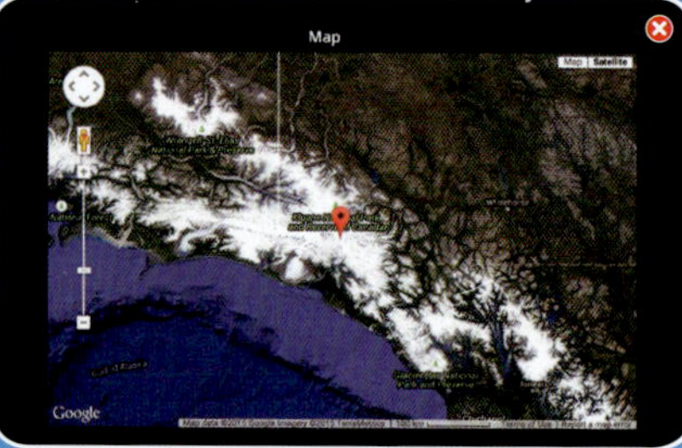

WEBLINKS

SLIDESHOWS

QUIZZES

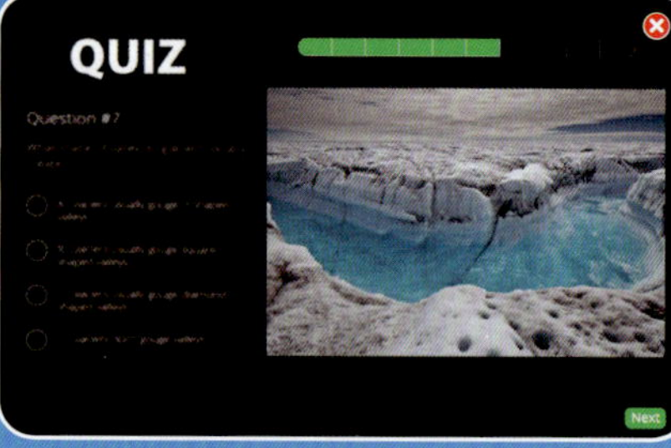

OPTIMIZED FOR

- ✓ TABLETS
- ✓ WHITEBOARDS
- ✓ COMPUTERS
- ✓ AND MUCH MORE!

Published by Lightbox Learning
276 5th Avenue
Suite 704 #917
New York, NY 10001
Website: www.openlightbox.com

First published by Cherry Lake Publishing in 2012

Library of Congress Control Number: 2021939459

ISBN 978-1-5105-5568-6 (hardcover)
ISBN 978-1-5105-5569-3 (multi-user eBook)

Printed in Guangzhou, China
1 2 3 4 5 6 7 8 9 0 25 24 23 22 21

082021
111020

Project Coordinator John Willis
Designer Jean Faye Marie Rodriguez

Photo Credits
Every reasonable effort has been made to trace ownership and to obtain permission to reprint copyright material. The publisher would be pleased to have any errors or omissions brought to its attention so that they may be corrected in subsequent printings.

The publisher acknowledges Getty Images as its primary image supplier for this title.